Facing Mighty Fears
About Throwing Up

Dr. Dawn's Mini Books About Mighty Fears
By Dawn Huebner, PhD
Illustrated by Liza Stevens
Helping children ages 6–10 live happier lives

Facing Mighty Fears About Health
ISBN 978 1 78775 928 2
eISBN 978 1 78775 927 5

Facing Mighty Fears About Animals
ISBN 978 1 78775 946 6
eISBN 978 1 78775 947 3

Facing Mighty Fears About Trying New Things
ISBN 978 1 78775 950 3
eISBN 978 1 78775 951 0

Watch for future titles in the
Dr. Dawn's Mini Books About Mighty Fears series.

Facing Mighty Fears
About Throwing Up

Dawn Huebner, PhD

Illustrated by Liza Stevens

Jessica Kingsley Publishers
London and Philadelphia

First published in Great Britain in 2022 by Jessica Kingsley Publishers
An imprint of Hodder & Stoughton Ltd
An Hachette Company

1

Copyright © Dawn Huebner 2022
Illustrations copyright © Liza Stevens 2022

A CIP catalogue record for this title is available from the
British Library and the Library of Congress

ISBN 978 1 78775 925 1
eISBN 978 1 78775 926 8

Printed and bound in Great Britain by TJ Books Limited

Jessica Kingsley Publishers' policy is to use papers that are natural,
renewable, and recyclable products and made from wood grown in
sustainable forests. The logging and manufacturing processes are expected
to conform to the environmental regulations of the country of origin.

Jessica Kingsley Publishers
Carmelite House
50 Victoria Embankment
London EC4Y 0DZ

www.jkp.com

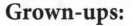

Grown-ups:

Need ideas about how to use this book?

Please see Dr. Dawn's
Note to Parents and Caregivers
on page 69.

You'll also find a **Resource Section**
highlighting books, websites, and organizations
for parents of anxious kids.

Why would anyone want to read a book about throwing up?

Throwing up is smelly and unpleasant.

It's

DISGUSTING,

DISTASTEFUL,

disagreeable,

DREADFUL.

Throwing up is certainly not something we choose to do, yet most of us end up doing it, at least once in a while.

If you happen to be a child who is fascinated by puke, you're in the right place. There's plenty that's fascinating here.

FUN FACT
Most people can't tell the difference between the smell of vomit and the smell of Parmesan cheese. A scientist did a study in which she had people smell butyric acid (the main smell in vomit). When they were told it was Parmesan cheese, they happily sniffed it in. When they were told it was vomit, they said it smelled terrible and didn't want to go near it!

FUN FACT
There are empty vomit bags on the moon. US astronauts Neil Armstrong and Buzz Aldrin would have left actual spew on the moon when they left behind other garbage, but no one threw up on their trip.

And, if you are the opposite—if you hate everything associated with throwing up and would rather throw this book across the room—you are in the right place, too.

How can that be?

How can one book be right for both puke-lovers and puke-haters?

Well, there's a saying that goes:

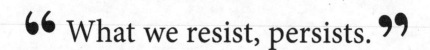

66 What we resist, persists. 99

Resist (verb)
To deny, push away, fight vigorously against.

Persist (verb)
To stick around, stay stubbornly in place.

This means that the more we avoid thinking about throwing up, the more thoughts about throwing up will follow us around.

The more desperately we try to push those thoughts away, the more stubbornly the thoughts will hold on.

Ugh. The last thing any of us wants is to have a brain full of puke thoughts.

BLOW CHUNKS

YACK

ralph

gush

get sick

EMIT

feed the fish

puke

upchuck

RETCH

eject

rainbow shower

un-eat

vom-cano

erupt

hurl

HEAVE

toss your cookies

liquid scream

BARF

URK

SPEW

VOMIT

be sick

SPIT UP

So, how can you get your puke thoughts to go away?

Well, if you stop resisting—if you let yourself think about, talk about, even joke about throwing up— your fear will no longer **PERSIST**.

Instead, it will fade away.

It's funny how that works.

To be able to stop thinking about something (like throwing up), you have to stop trying to *not* think about it.

Instead, you have to think about it. On purpose.
A lot.

You have to learn about it and talk about it and laugh about it and get used to it, so you can get to the point of not being so bothered by it.

You have to walk towards your fear rather than away from it. Face it to get rid of it.

So, here we go.

We're going to face puke.

But we're going to start slowly, by talking about something that isn't disgusting at all.

Something that's actually quite wonderful:

Bodies!

Bodies!

BODIES!

Bodies!

Bodies!

Bodies!

Bodies!

Everyone has a body, although
not all bodies are the same.

Some bodies are tall or short.
Lean or curvy. Dark or light
or a shade that's in between.

But none of that matters, because every body—no matter the shape, the size, the color—can do all sorts of wonderful things.

Mostly, we don't think about our bodies.

We don't sit around studying our ankles or noticing the movement of our chin.

We don't re-count our fingers each day or check to make sure our elbows still bend.

We don't think about the way our eyes blink.

Or consider the way our mouths slurp and chew
and giggle and spit and blow and whisper and sing.

We don't notice the way our toes wiggle and point
and spread and balance.

Or marvel at the way our skin—this flexible,
repairable stuff—holds us all together.

We take our bodies for granted, which means that
we trust them to do what they need to do without
paying attention to the details.

Even if one part of your body doesn't work the same as other people's bodies, **your** body is still amazing.

Your brain, and your body, and the people who care about you find clever ways to get things done.

Sometimes, we have to tell our bodies what to do.

But mostly they hum along on their own, breathing and blinking and swallowing and digesting without any instruction from us.

That's good.

It would be annoying if you had to tell your body every single thing it needed to do.

It's a good thing we're not designed that way. That there are certain things our bodies just do, on their own, without any instruction from us.

It's like that with all the basic things our bodies do to keep us alive:

Breathing

Sleeping

Swallowing

ELIMINATING

Let's talk about that last thing: eliminating.

Eliminate (verb)
To completely remove or get rid of something.

You've been eliminating since you were a baby. Everyone has.

From the day you are born until you are very, very old, your body takes the extra parts of the foods you eat and the liquids you drink—the parts you don't need—and gets rid of them.

It's pretty remarkable, actually.

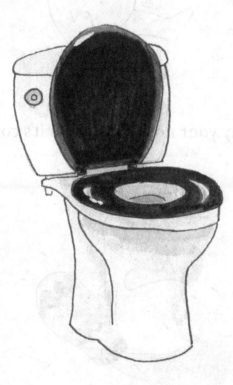

Sometimes our bodies eliminate things in a gentle, drippy way, like the way a baby drools...

...or the way your nose runs when it's cold out.

Sometimes we eliminate things more vigorously.

We **EXPEL** them.

Expel (verb)
To get rid of something forcefully.

> <u>My body's favorite ways to expel things:</u>
>
> _____
>
> * <u>Passing gas</u>   * <u>Burping</u>
> * <u>Sneezing</u>   * <u>Throwing up.</u>

Yup.

There it is.

Throwing up.

We're finally back to talking about that, because throwing up is one of the ways our bodies expel the things we don't need.

FUN FACT

Birds of prey—like owls or hawks—regurgitate pellets made of undigested bone, fur, and feathers to rid themselves of the parts of their prey they can't digest. After they throw up these pellets, they are ready to eat again.

FUN FACT

Cats groom themselves by licking, then they puke up clumpy hairballs. They feel so much better after gacking out these slimy hairballs.

Maybe "throwing up" isn't what you call it. That's okay. There are LOTS of words that mean the same thing:

hurl

get sick

gush

BARF

ralph

VOMIT

YACK

be sick

feed the fish

SPEW

RETCH

BLOW CHUNKS

upchuck

toss your cookies

eject

URK

vom-cano

HEAVE

puke

erupt

rainbow shower

un-eat

EMIT

liquid scream

SPIT UP

FUN FACT
The word "puke" was first used in the 16th century, by the now-famous bard, William Shakespeare.

Sometimes we throw up because we've eaten too much and our bodies can't handle all the food we've taken in.

Sometimes we throw up because we've been exposed to germs, and our bodies need to empty themselves so we can get back to feeling better.

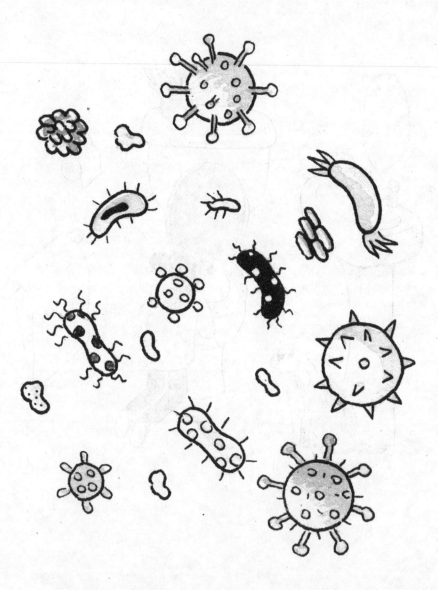

Sometimes we throw up because we are allergic to something we've eaten, or sensitive to it.

It's as if the food doesn't agree with us, and our body needs to get rid of it.

Sometimes we throw up because we are super excited.

Or because we've been bouncing around.

Or our bodies get confused and decide to clear out, just in case.

There are lots of reasons for throwing up, especially when we are young and our bodies are still figuring out how to do things.

FUN FACT
Snakes vomit for the same reasons people do, including nerves.

But as we get older, our bodies get better at handling upsets:

Too much food

Too much motion

Too much stress

TOO MANY GERMS

and we throw up less and less.

FUN FACT
Wolf pups lick their parents' mouths to get the adult wolf to throw up. They then gobble down their parents' vomit—a tasty treat for young pups.

But for everyone, throwing up sometimes happens. It just does.

Throwing up can feel scary.

It's uncomfortable. And messy. And embarrassing if you aren't at home.

Once throwing up starts, you can't really stop it, and that feels awful, too.

But even though it feels bad, throwing up isn't dangerous.

FUN FACT
Hyenas love to roll in vomit.

Some kids' brains make a mistake about that.

Some kids' brains think, "THROWING UP!?!?!? That's the worst thing ever!"

And for those kids, the possibility of throwing up becomes a big deal.

There's a name for this: emetophobia.

Emetophobia (noun)
(e-met-o-pho-bia)
An intense fear of
throwing up.

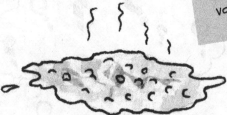

FUN FACT
Puke comes in lots of
colors. If you haven't
eaten for a while, your
vomit might be clear.

Kids who have emetophobia try to protect themselves from throwing up.

They avoid the foods they ate the last time they threw up.

They stay away from the clothes they were wearing, and the things that they touched.

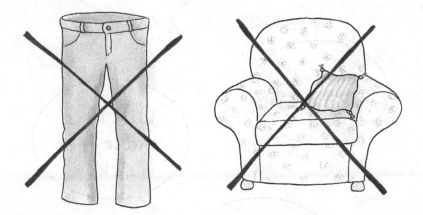

They don't go near anyone who has been sick, or might be sick, or could get sick.

They ask for reassurance that they aren't going to be sick.

Can you feel my forehead?

Is this healthy?

Will I be okay?

Will this make me sick?

Do I have a fever?

Kids with emetophobia don't want to even **think** about throwing up, and yet they end up thinking about it all the time.

BLOW CHUNKS

YACK

ralph

gush   get sick   EMIT

feed the fish   puke   upchuck

RETCH

eject   rainbow shower

un-eat

vom-cano   erupt   hurl

HEAVE

toss your cookies

liquid scream   BARF   URK

SPEW   VOMIT

be sick   SPIT UP

But the thing is, it doesn't matter if you think about
throwing up or not.

Or if you eat certain foods or not (unless you
are truly allergic to those foods, and then it
does matter).

Or if you wear the clothes you threw up in or not.

If your body needs to throw up, it's going to
throw up.

That's just the way it is.

PUKE HAPPENS.

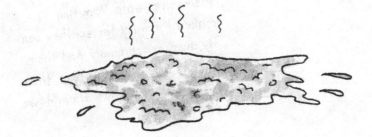

And it's good, actually. It's good to throw up.

Because even though it's yucky while it's happening, it helps our bodies get back on track.

We throw up, and then we're done and we start to feel better.

FUN FACT
Butterfly caterpillars throw up green puke that smells and tastes bad, which keeps predators like birds away.

FUN FACT
Turkey vultures vomit to keep themselves safe. Vomiting makes them lighter so they can fly away more easily. And their puke is acidic, which stings their predators and slows them down.

Sometimes there's more your body needs to get rid of, and you'll throw up again.

But whether you puke one time, or three times, or five or six times, eventually the throwing up will stop and you'll start to feel better.

Someone will clean things up, and help you find a place to rest.

If you aren't at home, the grown-ups around you will help you get there.

Once you are home, you'll get to put on comfy clothes and snuggle on a couch or in your bed.

FUN FACT
Honey is bee barf.

You might get to read a good book or watch one of your favorite shows.

Maybe you'll want to sleep.

Or maybe you'll feel totally fine and be ready to continue your day.

Either way, it will be just a brief YUCK, and you'll deal with it, and life will go on.

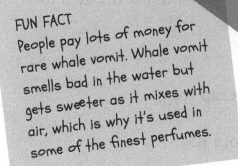

FUN FACT
People pay lots of money for rare whale vomit. Whale vomit smells bad in the water but gets sweeter as it mixes with air, which is why it's used in some of the finest perfumes.

So, to help your brain realize that puke happens, and it's not that big a deal, here's what you need to do...

Step 1

1. Find your favorite word for throwing up. There are LOTS of words to choose from.

Every day, repeat your favorite word. Say it lots of times.

→ Use the word in a rap song.

→ Write a poem about it.

→ Pretend it's a tongue-twister and say it 20 times fast.

puke

gush

get sick

ralph

BARF

YACK

Then choose another word and do it all again.

VOMIT

be sick

feed the fish

SPEW

RETCH

BLOW CHUNKS

upchuck

toss your cookies

eject

vom-cano

HEAVE

URK

erupt

rainbow shower

EMIT

un-eat

hurl

liquid scream

SPIT UP

Make your puke word into a beautiful poster to hang in your room.

Use index cards to create a Go Fish deck with all your "favorite" vomit words.

Play "Go Puke" by asking, "Do you have a Spew?" "Do you have an Upchuck?" "Do you have Vomit?"

Be creative.

Find ways to sing about, draw about, and act out throwing up. Make it goofy. Make it gross. Do it again and again.

FUN FACT

Houseflies barf onto their own food to break the food down and make it easier to digest. Yum yum.

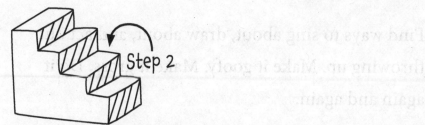

Step 2

2. **Whenever you start to feel afraid, tell yourself, "If I get sick, I get sick, and then I'll feel better."**

If I get sick, I get sick, and then I'll feel better.

If I get sick, I get sick, and then I'll feel better.

If I get sick, I get sick, and then I'll feel better.

If I get sick, I get sick, and then I'll feel better.

If I get sick, I get sick, and then I'll feel better.

If I get sick, I get sick, and then I'll feel better.

If I get sick, I get sick, and then I'll feel better.

If I get sick, I get sick, and then I'll feel better.

If I get sick, I get sick, and then I'll feel better.

If I get sick, I get sick, and then I'll feel better.

If I get sick, I get sick, and then I'll feel better.

If I get sick, I get sick, and then I'll feel better.

If I get sick, I get sick, and then I'll feel better.

You may be tempted to tell yourself, "I'm not going to throw up!"

> I'm not going to throw up!

You may want your parents to tell you, "You're not going to throw up."

> You're not going to throw up.

It may seem as if this kind of reassurance is helpful, but it isn't.

Your brain needs to get used to the idea that puke happens, and that it's not a big deal.

Re-read this book if you need to. Then, make a notecard that says, "If I get sick, I get sick, and then I'll feel better."

Read the notecard to yourself, then read it out loud.

Read it over and over again, day after day after day. Until you've memorized the sentence. Until you can say it and actually start believing it.

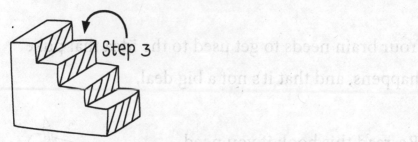

Step 3

3. Challenge yourself to do the things you are avoiding.

→ Wear the clothes that feel risky.

→ Touch the things you aren't touching.

→ Eat the foods you ate the last time you threw up.

→ Go to the places that remind you of throwing up.

Start by making a list of all the things you've been avoiding, the things you associate with throwing up.

Turn your list into a set of challenges, and start doing them one by one.

Don't do extreme things to avoid throwing up.
Extreme things don't actually protect you. They
only keep you focused on your fear.

Instead, make your way through
your list of challenges.

My challenges:

✓ Sit on edge of couch	Eat mac and cheese
✓ Lie on couch	Go back to restaurant
✓ Wear green socks for a minute	Stop taking temperature
✓ Wear green socks all day	Put bucket back in closet
Put on blue leggings	Don't ask if I'm okay

If you need to, you can read another book about managing worry, or ask your parents to help you find a therapist to teach you how to do challenges like these even though you feel afraid.

There are ideas about additional books you and your parents can read, and websites your parents can visit, at the end of this book.

You can learn to manage your fear.

Following all three steps is a great way to start.

1. Find your favorite puke word and use it creatively.

2. Tell yourself, "If I get sick, I get sick, and then I'll feel better."

3. Challenge yourself to do the things you are avoiding.

No one likes to throw up.

No one likes to see other people throwing up.

But everyone, everyone, everyone pukes—
at least sometimes.

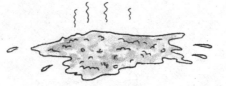

Everyone pukes.

And someday, you will, too.

And then it will be over.

And you can get on with your life.

▽▽▽▽▽▽▽▽▽▽
Note to Parents and Caregivers
△△△△△△△△△△

No one likes to throw up. No one likes to see it, smell it, experience it, or clean it. But emetophobia (the fear of throwing up) is different. It's an intense, persistent fear that gets in the way, making it hard to eat, sleep, go places, and do things. Interestingly, even though many people have never heard of it, emetophobia is one of the most common fears for children. Adults, too.

This book is a good starting point for children with emetophobia. Know that your child is likely to resist reading it, though. The mere mention of throwing up sends emetophobic children into a tailspin. So, you may need to go slowly: having your child get used to simply being in the same room as the book, then looking at the cover, then flipping through the pages.

There's a technique called "exposure," which is the capstone of treatment for all phobias (intense persistent fears). Exposure means facing the thing you are afraid of. On purpose. Repeatedly.

It is often combined with something called "desensitization," which means getting used to something a little bit at a time. So, your child may need to desensitize to this book before actually reading it. That's okay.

You might decide to play hide-the-book with your child before actually reading it (you hide the book and your child finds it, then switch roles). You might challenge your child to flip through the book trying to spot particular words you call out: "Find the word *the*", "Find the word *baby*." Or read some of the fun facts together before reading the text. You may need to read part of the book and then pause. Do return, though. The book is brief, and exposure is built in so children will benefit from reading and re-reading, even if it's only a section at a time.

If your child is significantly affected by emetophobia, you might consider using this book in combination with therapy. And if you, yourself, have a fear of throwing up, you will undoubtedly benefit from the steady presence of a therapist guiding you and your child through the book and additional practice activities. There is a list of resources at the end of this book.

Some additional tips

1. Do what you can to stay calm in the face of your child's rising panic, including when they think they might throw up. Remind yourself that your child is scared but—even if they do throw up—they are not in danger. Empathize with your child, saying things like, "I know. This feels scary to you." Then express faith in your child's ability to cope, "I know you can get through this." Keep your own breathing steady. Your calm sends a message to the primitive part of your child's brain that is on the lookout for danger. Your calm signals safety.

2. Avoid repeated reassurances. You and your child are likely to be well versed in this particular dance. Your child asks, "Will this make me sick?" (or some version of that question) and you answer, "You're fine; you're not going to get sick!" (or some version of that answer). The reassurance dance needs to stop. Reassurance helps your child only for a moment but keeps them locked into needing to know with absolute certainty that they aren't going to throw up, and they can't know that. None of us can. So, when your child asks, "Will this make me sick?" your answer needs to be, "I don't know."

   This will not be easy for you or your child, but it is for the best. Saying you don't know is the truth. You don't have a crystal ball, so you can't possibly know whether or not your child will throw up. You can make a good guess, but good guesses are never enough for anxious children; anxiety craves certainty.

   Your child needs to get used to and come to accept the possibility of throwing up. That's what this whole book is about, and that's what the successful treatment of emetophobia rests on: the fact that someday your child will throw up, and that's okay.

3. Stop participating in your child's avoidance. This one is challenging, too. Your child insists that you pick them up from the sleepover, or that you serve them only cheese sticks and pretzels, or that you keep their red shirt clean because that's the only shirt that feels safe to them—and you do those things because you love your child, and you see that they are suffering. But these are short-term fixes that keep the problem going in the long run. Avoidance locks worry in place. Instead, help

your child learn to move towards the things that scare them, the things linked through coincidence to the last time they threw up, or someone else threw up.

Vomiting is unpleasant. It looks bad, smells bad, tastes bad, feels bad. Nothing is going to change that. But what can change—what will change if you and your child are persistent—is the way your child's brain reacts to the possibility of throwing up. It can become something like stubbing their toe, an experience no one wants but few of us focus on or fear.

You can do this. Your child can do this. I'll be rooting for you.

Dr. Dawn

Resources

Organizations

These organizations provide information about childhood anxiety, and include therapist locators to assist with finding specialized care:

USA

The Anxiety and Depression Association of America:
https://adaa.org

The International OCD Foundation:
https://iocdf.org

UK

Anxiety UK:
www.anxietyuk.org.uk

Young Minds:
https://youngminds.org.uk

AU/NZ

Beyond Blue:
www.beyondblue.org.au

Kids Health:
https://kidshealth.org.nz

Please also reach out to your child's pediatrician for names of local providers.

Web-based resources

https://library.jkp.com
Dr. Dawn's Seven-Step Solution for When Worry Takes
Over: Easy-to-Implement Strategies for Parents or Carers of
Anxious Kids, see page 78.
Video Training Course

www.anxioustoddlers.com
Natasha Daniels of AT Parenting Survival creates podcasts,
blog posts, and free resources about anxiety. She also offers
subscription courses, coaching, and treatment.

https://childmind.org
This NY Institute offers articles on a host of topics, including
anxiety, with a unique "Ask an Expert" feature providing
trustworthy, relatable advice.

https://copingskillsforkids.com
Janine Halloran provides free, easy-to-implement, child-friendly tips on calming anxiety, managing stress, and more.

https://emetophobiahelp.org
Anna Christie is a one-time sufferer, now tireless champion of the effective treatment of emetophobia. Her website has a comprehensive collection of words, still pictures, and videos perfect for exposure treatment. And she offers online coaching.

https://gozen.com
Kid-tested, therapist-approved, highly effective animated videos teaching skills related to anxiety, resilience, emotional intelligence, and more.

www.worrywisekids.org
Tamar Chansky of WorryWiseKids provides a treasure-trove of information for parents of anxious children.

Recommended reading

There are many appealing, effective books to help children manage worries and fears. Please check with your preferred bookseller, who can guide you towards books particularly suited to your child's needs. Here are a few suggestions.

For younger children

What to Do When You Worry Too Much: A Kid's Guide to Overcoming Anxiety by Dawn Huebner, PhD, American Psychological Association.

Binnie the Baboon Anxiety and Stress Activity Book by Dr. Karen Treisman, Jessica Kingsley Publishers.

Hey Warrior: A Book for Kids about Anxiety by Karen Young, Little Steps Publishing.

Little Meerkat's Big Panic: A Story About Learning New Ways to Feel Calm by Jane Evans, Jessica Kingsley Publishers.

The Nervous Knight: A Story About Overcoming Worries and Anxiety by Anthony Lloyd Jones, Jessica Kingsley Publishers.

Starving the Anxiety Gremlin for Children Aged 5–9: A CBT Workbook on Anxiety Management by Kate Collins-Donnelly, Jessica Kingsley Publishers.

For older children

Outsmarting Worry: An Older Kid's Guide to Managing Anxiety by Dawn Huebner, PhD, Jessica Kingsley Publishers.

All Birds Have Anxiety by Kathy Hoopmann, Jessica Kingsley Publishers.

The Can-Do Kid's Journal: Discover Your Confidence Superpower! by Sue Atkins, Jessica Kingsley Publishers.

Can I Tell You About Anxiety? A Guide for Friends and Family by Lucy Willetts, Jessica Kingsley Publishers.

Doodle Your Worries Away: A CBT Doodling Workbook for Kids Who Feel Worried or Anxious by Tanja Sharpe, Jessica Kingsley Publishers.

Help! I've Got an Alarm Bell Going Off in My Head! How Panic, Anxiety and Stress Affect Your Body by K.L. Aspden, Jessica Kingsley Publishers.

The Panicosaurus: Managing Anxiety in Children, Including those with Asperger Syndrome by K.L. Al-Ghani, Jessica Kingsley Publishers.

Starving the Anxiety Gremlin: A CBT Workbook on Anxiety Management for Young People Aged 10+ by Kate Collins-Donnelly, Jessica Kingsley Publishers.

For parents

Anxious Kids, Anxious Parents by Dr. Reid Wilson and Lynn Lyons, Health Communications Inc.

The A–Z of Therapeutic Parenting: Strategies and Solutions by Sarah Naish, Jessica Kingsley Publishers.

Breaking Free of Child Anxiety and OCD: A Scientifically Proven Program for Parents by Eli R. Lebowitz, PhD, Oxford University Press.

The No Worries Guide to Raising Your Anxious Child by Karen Lynn Cassiday, Jessica Kingsley Publishers.

Parenting Your Anxious Toddler by Natasha Daniels, Jessica Kingsley Publishers.

Peaceful Parent, Happy Kids by Dr. Laura Markham, TarcherPerigee.

The Yes Brain: How to Cultivate Courage, Curiosity and Resilience in Your Child by Dr. Dan Siegel and Dr. Tina Payne Bryson, Bantam Press.

Dr. Dawn's
SEVEN-STEP SOLUTION FOR WHEN WORRY TAKES OVER

Easy-to-Implement Strategies for Parents or Carers of Anxious Kids

worry has a way of turning into WORRY in the blink of an eye. This upper-case WORRY causes children to fret about unlikely scenarios and shrink away from routine challenges, ultimately holding entire families hostage. But upper-case WORRY is predictable and manageable once you understand its tricks.

This 7-video series will help you recognize WORRY's tricks while teaching a handful of techniques to help you and your child break free.

Each video contains learning objectives and action steps along with need-to-know content presented in a clear, engaging manner by child psychologist and best-selling author, Dr. Dawn Huebner. The videos are available from https://library.jkp.com.

Video One: Trolling for Danger (time 8:15)

- The role of the amygdala in spotting and alerting us to danger
- What happens when the amygdala sets off an alarm
- Real dangers versus false alarms
- Calming the brain (yours and your child's) to get back to thinking

Video Two: The Worry Loop (time 10:15)

- The "loop" that keeps Worry in place
- How to identify where your child is in the Worry Loop

Video Three: Externalizing Anxiety (time 11:41)

- Externalizing anxiety as a powerful first step
- Talking back to Worry
- Teaching your child to talk back to Worry
- Talking back without entering into a debate

Video Four: Calming the Brain and Body (time 13:36)

- Breathing techniques
- Mindfulness techniques
- Distraction techniques
- Which technique (how to choose)?

Video Five: Getting Rid of Safety Behaviors (time 15:18)

- Preparation
- The role of exposure
- Explaining exposure to your child
- Creating an exposure hierarchy

Video Six: Worrying Less Is Not the Goal (time 13:02)

- The more you fight anxiety, the more it holds on
- The more you accommodate anxiety, the more it stays
- Anxiety is an error message, a false alarm
- When you stop letting Worry be in charge, it fades

Video Seven: Putting It All Together (time 19:42)

- A review of the main techniques
- Deciding where to start
- The role of rewards
- Supporting your child, not Worry